Is the Reverse Mortgage a Scam? Or a Good Idea?

Amelia Rojas

The Reverse Mortgage. Scam or a good idea?

PUT ME ON
The Do Not Call List
YOU SCAMMER!

The Reverse Mortgage. Scam or a good idea?

The Reverse Mortgage. Scam or a good idea?

Copyright © 2023 Amelia Rojas

All rights reserved.

Printed in The United States of America

First Edition, 2023

ISBN: 9798374255195

DISCLAIMER

I am not a financial advisor or attorney. The content in this book is based on my experience as a former licensed Reverse Mortgage Loan Officer, as well as conversations with seniors seeking information about Reverse Mortgages.

The information provided is not intended to override lender guidelines or serve as legal or financial advice. I am not affiliated with, or endorsed by, any government agency or financial institution.

If you are considering a Reverse Mortgage, it's important to consult with trusted family members, an attorney, or a financial planner. Remember, a Reverse Mortgage—also known as a Home Equity Conversion Mortgage—is still a mortgage, with both benefits and risks, just like any other loan. This book is meant to provide a general overview to help you make an informed decision. While it may contain factual information, it is largely based on my personal opinions and experiences, and may include some bias.

CONTENTS

INTRODUCTION 6

WHAT IS A REVERSE MORTGAGE? 7

NO MONTHLY PAYMENT IS REQUIRED 8

REVERSE MORTGAGE FACTS 9

IS THE REVERSE MORTGAGE A SCAM? 10

IS THE REVERSE MORTGAGE A GOOD IDEA? 12

REVERSE MORTGAGE RISKS 13

WHAT OPTIONS WILL THE HEIRS HAVE? 14

REVERSE MORTGAGE LENDER SEARCH 15

WHAT TO EXPECT FROM A LOAN OFFICER 16

COMPLIANCE AND SCRIPTS 17

QUESTIONS TO ASK 18

IMPORTANT EXPIRATION DATES 20

REQUIRED LOAN DOCUMENTS 21

FILE COMPLAINTS OR REPORT VIOLATIONS 22

DO NOT CALL LIST 23

CONCLUSION 24

SUGGESTIONS FOR FURTHER RESEARCH 25

ABOUT THE AUTHOR 26

INTRODUCTION

I am a former Licensed Reverse Mortgage Loan Officer with experience in the industry.

While I do not claim to know everything, I have had numerous conversations with seniors seeking information about Reverse Mortgages, and I've learned a lot along the way.
In this book, I will share insights based on those conversations and my experiences. One thing I learned is that some love Reverse Mortgages, some have reservations, and others think they are a scam. There are a lot of misconceptions out there, and everyone has their own perspective.
My goal is not to steer you one way or the other but to provide you with facts and tips to help you decide if a Reverse Mortgage is right for you.

I will keep it simple and straightforward.

Remember, do your due diligence. Consult with trusted family members, an attorney, or a financial planner to get a well-rounded view. Do not rely solely on my opinion—gather information from multiple sources to make the best decision for you.

Failure to meet obligations could result in foreclosure.

WHAT IS A REVERSE MORTGAGE?

Let's get the basics out of the way.

A Reverse Mortgage, also known as a Home Equity Conversion Mortgage (HECM), is a government-insured loan for homeowners aged 62 or older. It allows you to access a portion of your home's equity without monthly mortgage payments. However, you cannot access 100% of your home's equity.

To qualify, you must meet certain requirements, including:

- Age requirement
- Property type requirements
- Equity requirements
- Occupancy requirements
- Condition of the home requirements
- Financial Assessment requirements

Homeowners have some obligations—they must continue paying property taxes, homeowners' insurance, and maintain the home. The loan becomes due when you sell, move out, or pass away. Failure to meet these obligations could result in foreclosure.

NO MONTHLY PAYMENT IS REQUIRED

Yes, it is true, with a Reverse Mortgage loan, there is no required monthly mortgage payment, and the loan is not due and payable, as long as the borrowers:

- Continue to live in the home as your primary residence.
- Continue to pay for Homeowner's Insurance.
- Continue to pay Property Taxes.
- Continue to pay for HOA if applicable.
- Continue to upkeep the home to FHA standards.

Most of the seniors I spoke with used the Reverse Mortgage to eliminate their mortgage payments because they found themselves in financial hardship, could not make ends meet, and had no other options.

In summary, yes—it's true that no monthly mortgage payment is required. However, if the homeowners fail to meet the mandatory obligations, the loan may become due immediately and could lead to foreclosure.

REVERSE MORTGAGE FACTS

Fact #1:
The HECM is a Non-Recourse Loan.
If the loan balance is higher than your home's value, your heirs will not be on the hook for the difference. They can choose to sell the home or refinance, and they will not owe more than the home's value. This feature ensures your loved ones are not burdened with debt beyond the home's worth.

Fact #2:
The Financial Assessment
This is not optional—it is required. It's used to determine if you can continue paying property taxes, homeowners' insurance, and other necessary expenses. If it is found that you cannot, a Life Expectancy Set-Aside (LESA) may be needed. Think of it as an escrow account, funded from the loan proceeds, which reduces the available funds for you.

Fact #3:
Repayment of the Reverse Mortgage Loan
The loan becomes due when the last borrower sells the home, moves out, or passes away. It may also become due if you fail to pay property taxes, homeowners' insurance, or if the home's condition declines and necessary repairs are not made. In such cases, the loan becomes due immediately.

IS THE REVERSE MORTGAGE A SCAM?

First, there are hundreds of scams, and seniors are often targeted. Be careful who you share your personal information with.

When in doubt—online, STOP! Don't click. On the phone, STOP! Hang up!

To help you decide: The Reverse Mortgage is just a mortgage. It is insured by the FHA and designed for seniors to access some of their home's equity without making monthly payments.

Seniors often ask, "What's the catch?" There is no catch. It's simply a mortgage, and lenders make money just like with other mortgage loans.

It is important to research any lender you are considering. Some fraudsters target seniors, so ensure the lender is reputable. Check their standing with the Better Business Bureau, read customer reviews, and verify their credentials. Be wary of unsolicited offers and high-pressure sales tactics.

Always consult with a trusted Financial Advisor or HUD-approved housing counselor before making decisions.

So, is it a Scam? No. It is a legitimate mortgage loan.

ALTERNATIVES TO A REVERSE MORTGAGE

Most seniors I spoke with were no longer able to work for various reasons, such as health, and their only source of Income was Social Security Income, and they were struggling to make ends meet and were considering the Reverse Mortgage.

If you find yourself in a similar situation, I encourage you to explore all available options.

- Reach out to your family, they may be able to help.
- Consult with a Financial Advisor for financial advice.
- Consult with an Attorney for legal advice.
- Sell the house and downsize to a smaller home.
- Consult with a Licensed Reverse Mortgage Specialist.
- Obtain a Reverse Mortgage proposal to compare.

A written Reverse Mortgage proposal is a great place to start, the numbers do not lie, and you can share it and review it with your Financial Advisor, Attorney, and family, and decide together.

A reputable Loan Officer is not going to object to this, instead, they will gladly answer any questions, even schedule a time to speak with your Financial Planner or family members.

IS THE REVERSE MORTGAGE A GOOD IDEA?

The Reverse Mortgage is not for everyone, and not everyone qualifies. It is important to understand that this type of loan has a growing balance with certain benefits and risks.

This is a financial decision you should not be making alone, and I highly recommend that you speak with your family or other trusted individuals regarding this decision. You will go through the typical loan hoops, like completing an application, getting your credit pulled, signing lots of documents, gathering required documents, getting Reverse Mortgage Counseling, and getting your home appraised, and this process could take months to complete.

So, is the Reverse Mortgage a good idea? That depends on your situation, and I recommend speaking with a Reverse Mortgage professional for a consultation.

If anyone answers those questions quickly without knowing anything about your specific scenario, I will say they are not doing their job.

REVERSE MORTGAGE RISKS

Growing Loan Balance:
By borrowing against your home's equity without making monthly mortgage payments, your loan balance increases over time due to accruing interest and FHA mortgage insurance. Some homeowners are not concerned about the growing loan balance; they figure it will be paid off after they die, and it is not a deciding factor. However, it is important to consider that the loan balance may affect the ability of their heirs to keep the home.

Could you lose your home?
As with any mortgage loan, there is a potential risk of foreclosure due to defaulting on the loan. You might be thinking, well, how could I default on the loan if there is no required mortgage payment? So, here is how. The Reverse Mortgage loan agreement requires that the borrower lives in the home permanently and pays for their mandatory obligations as mentioned previously.

Contact an Attorney for legal advice if this is your case.

WHAT OPTIONS WILL THE HEIRS HAVE?

Heirs have options:
They can pay off the HECM loan balance with their own money, refinance the loan into their name, or sell the home.

Selling the home:
Most heirs select this option. They contact the mortgage servicer and inform them of their intent to sell. The heirs will then contact a Real Estate Agent and put the house up for sale. Once the house is sold, the Reverse Mortgage balance is paid through the sale of the home, and if there is any remaining equity, it goes to the heirs. If the balance is more than the home is worth, they do not have to pay the difference; that's when the FHA Non-recourse loan rule goes into effect. They will not be on the hook for the difference.

How long do the heirs have to sell the house?
Contact the Reverse Mortgage Servicer for this information. Communication is key.

REVERSE MORTGAGE LENDER SEARCH

Word of Mouth Referral:
When searching for a Reverse Mortgage Lender, nothing beats a referral from someone you know, for the obvious reason that it is someone they trust and like.

In the absence of a referral, I suggest you check these sources:

- HUD Online Lender Approved Search List
- BBB Ratings and Complaints
- NMLS Resource Center for Licensing
- NRMLA Reverse Mortgage Lenders Association.
- Google & Yelp Online Reviews
- Consumers Advocate Reviews

Ask questions and do not provide any personal information unless you are 100% sure that it is a reputable lender.

Most mortgage companies offer a variety of loan options, including reverse mortgages. However, I recommend selecting a lender that specializes in reverse mortgages. These loans have specific guidelines, so it's in your best interest to work with an experienced professional who focuses on reverse mortgages.

The Reverse Mortgage. Scam or a good idea?

WHAT TO EXPECT FROM A LOAN OFFICER

Once you have selected a Lender and you contact them, here is what you may expect from the Loan Officer.

The Loan Officer will provide you with their name and NMLS License number, so write it down.

A professional Reverse Mortgage Loan Officer will take the time to have an in-depth conversation with you to understand your goals and answer all your questions without rushing you or pressuring you and will refrain from fear tactics.

The Loan Officer will ask you questions about your:
- Age
- Goals, what are you looking to accomplish?
- Property Type
- Property Conditions
- Ownership
- Occupancy
- Estimated Value
- Current loan balance if you have one.
- Liens against the property
- Heirs and what they plan to do with the home.

The Financial Assessment is a requirement, and it may be completed during this initial conversation, which covers questions about your Income and Debts.

COMPLIANCE AND SCRIPTS

Reverse Mortgage Loan Officers undergo extensive training, hold a Mortgage License, and are required to adhere to many rules for compliance. The lender and loan officer face disciplinary action, fines, penalties, and even the loss of their license for prohibited acts and practices.

Recorded Lines:
When calling a Reverse Mortgage Lender, you may hear them say that they are on a "Recorded Line" this is part of their compliance, and it protects you. The Managers can pull calls to ensure the Loan Officer is compliant and provide you with accurate information that is not misleading.

Credit Pulling compliance script:
Before pulling your credit, the loan officer will request permission and read a compliance script. Again, only provide permission to someone you know, like, and trust.

Application HMDA compliance script:
The Home Mortgage Disclosure Act (HMDA) is a federal law requiring lenders to collect data to ensure compliance with anti-discrimination laws. You may be asked about your ethnicity, race, and sex (e.g., "Are you male or female?"). While these questions must be asked, you can decline to answer.
The reverse mortgage industry is built on compliance, so trust the specialist to follow all required procedures. A reputable professional will never cut corners.

QUESTIONS TO ASK

To avoid miscommunication, ask questions.

Suggested questions to ask:

- Is it possible to lose the home?
- What options will my heirs have?
- Will my loan balance grow?
- What if the loan balance exceeds the value of the home?
- Is my Interest Rate fixed or adjustable?
- What is my Interest Rate?
- Does the Adjustable Interest rate have a cap?
- What if I do not pay my property taxes?
- What if I do not pay for my homeowner's Insurance?

An experienced Reverse Mortgage Loan Officer will answer these questions without hesitation. If they don't, it might be time to consider a different lender.

What are my out-of-pocket expenses:

There are two out-of-pocket expenses, and they vary in cost.

1. Reverse Mortgage Counseling Fee
2. FHA Appraisal Fee

The rule of thumb is that borrower pays for the appraisal fee.

Do not allow a "free appraisal offer" to be your only reason for choosing a lender. That's not the most important thing.

Lender reputation, rating, and experience are far more important than a "free appraisal" offer or any other gimmicky promotion.

Please note, guidelines may have changed since the writing of this book, so it is essential to stay updated when making decisions.

IMPORTANT EXPIRATION DATES

Reverse Mortgage FHA Appraisal
4 months / 120 days

Reverse Mortgage Counseling Certificate
6 months/ 180 days

Credit Report
4 months/ 120 days

As a reminder the information here is not intended to override your lender's requirements, which may differ from my opinion, also different states have different requirements, or the information may have changed. This information is to provide you with a general overview.

REQUIRED LOAN DOCUMENTS

Like with any mortgage loan, you will be required to provide certain documents, here's a short list of some of the preliminary documents that you may be required to provide:

- Social Security Awards Letter (most recent)
- Copy of Social Security Card
- Copy of Government Issued ID
- Copy of Driver's License
- Mortgage statement (if applicable)

The Mortgage Underwriter will require that these documents be clear and legible.

This is not an all-inclusive list of required documents, and your Lender may require additional documents.

As a reminder only provide your information to trusted lenders to avoid potential Identity theft.

FILE COMPLAINTS OR REPORT VIOLATIONS

HECM loans Complaints or violations

U.S. Department of Housing and Urban Development
451 7th Street, SW
Washington, DC 20410
Telephone 800-225-5342

Federal Trade Commission
Consumer Response Center
600 Pennsylvania Avenue, NW
Washington, DC 205801
Telephone 877-382-4357

Credit Reporting Agencies - Fraud Alert

Experian
888-397-3742

TransUnion
800-680-7289

Equifax
800-525-6285

I am not affiliated with or endorsed by any of the above.

DO NOT CALL LIST

Did you go online to request information, and now the calls will not stop?

If so, guess what?

You'll probably get more calls than you expected.

Just remember—the representative is simply following up on the request you submitted.

There's no need to get angry or frustrated.

Just ask to be placed on the Do Not Call list.

That's the magic word—"DNC." They're required to comply.

CONCLUSION

Is the Reverse Mortgage a Scam?
No, it is not a scam. A reverse mortgage is a legitimate loan, and I hope I have provided enough information to help you make an informed decision.

Remember, a reverse mortgage is simply a mortgage—with specific requirements, benefits, and risks, just like any other loan. It is highly recommended that you consult with your family, as well as a financial advisor or planner, a licensed reverse mortgage specialist, or an attorney to help determine if it's the right choice for you.

If you decide to move forward, be sure to do your due diligence. Check reputable sources like the Better Business Bureau website and the FHA Online Lender List to ensure you are working with a trustworthy lender.

Ask plenty of questions and make sure you fully understand how the reverse mortgage works. And most importantly, never share your personal information unless you are 100% certain of the person's identity, to protect yourself from identity theft.

If you believe you have been a victim of identity theft, report it immediately.

Suggestions for Further Research

HUD Lender List – Find a HUD Approved Lender – www.hud.gov/program_offices/housing/sfh/lender/lender list

U.S. Department of Housing and Urban Development – www.hud.gov

Home Equity Conversion Mortgage for Seniors – www.hud.gov/program_offices/housing/sfh/hecm/hecm home

Better Business Bureau – BBB – Find Trusted BBB ratings, and consumer reviews – www.bbb.org

Nationwide Mortgage Licensing System - NMLS Resource Center – https://mortgage.nationwidelicensingsystem.org

Federal Trade Commission – FTC – Protecting America's Consumers – www.ftc.gov

Federal Trade Commission – National Do Not Call Registry – www.donotcall.gov

The National Reverse Mortgage Lenders Association – NRMLA – www.nrmlaonline.org

Consumers Advocate website – Lender Reviews – www.consumersadvocate.org

I am not affiliated with or endorsed by any of the above.

ABOUT THE AUTHOR

Amelia Rojas

Baby boomer born in 1964—mother, grandmother, and former Reverse Mortgage Loan Officer—who enjoys sharing valuable information that others may find helpful.

Contact
Dahmasbooks@gmail.com

Thank You!

I chose this little character because, being on the phone daily, I often heard this—due to many common misconceptions.

Thank you for reading, and I hope you found the information helpful!

The Reverse Mortgage. Scam or a good idea?

www.ingramcontent.com/pod-product-compliance
Lightning Source LLC
Chambersburg PA
CBHW050327220526
45465CB00005B/2169